INSANELY

Inspiring

WRITING PROMPTS FOR

LITTLES

BIGGLES BIGGLES

&

MIDDLES

By Stacey Lytle

"The most precious jewels you'll ever have around your neck are the arms of your children."

Dedicated to my most precious jewels . . .

Shealyn, Danielle, Myles, Bryce, Wyatt,

Cassandra, and Natalie

Contents

One

My Philosophy...

I believe that *everyone* has a story inside of them--there are times I feel I have a whole library. I also believe that anyone can learn to write well, or better than they have been. I believe anyone can find immense fulfillment in story-telling, and in their own way.

While I understand that not every person wants to become a writer, the fact is that every human on this planet will be required to write something--at some point--that will likely be shared with others. No matter how long we're on earth, we all have a contribution to make . . . even if it's only to live our own stories.

Knowing this, will we strive to embrace writing--and while we are at it--inspire others to do the same? Who knows? Maybe those who might not have experimented with writing might want the experience.

I believe that there is a place inside of us that is filled with unlimited amounts of genius, and that wonderful place can be found when we pull out a paper and pen and let nothing get in the way of expressing it! Writing is this magical place where you, as the writer, are 100% in control: if you can dream it, you can share it, and make it so. If you want to be somewhere or be something, write it--and have the adventure! If there is a dynamic character that you imagine--create it! If you long to walk the Cliffs of Moher in Ireland, fly in a hot-air balloon to Indonesia, or sail along the Mediterranean Coast, the French Riviera, or the Great Barrier Reef in Australia--take up paper, pen, or word-processor, and spell out the details of your fanciful voyage!

It's your story and you are in the driver's seat. That is the promise of embracing a life filled with creative writing--it's a part of the story of your life.

So, imagine . . .

What will your story be?

Two

WHY???

Why??? One of the biggest questions *ever!*

Why this? Why not something else?

Why, after 20 + years in education have I decided to share my ideas on writing?

Why do I have such unique views on the processes of writing?

Why am I not concerned *first* about spelling, punctuation and grammar?

Why do I believe that what I have to share can make a difference in the lives of others? In your life???

My first answer is that I feel it is a travesty that there are people that either despise the very thought of writing OR are terrified by the act of holding a pen and putting it to paper. Another concern, is that there are people who think they generally have nothing worthwhile to write or share.

On the other hand, there are those who may even have something on the Bestseller list, but could still find new, unanticipated ways to love writing.

And then, there's everyone in between.

Whether you have never written, or you write on a frequent basis, teach writing, are a blogger, or are an expert in the field . . . THIS BOOK IS FOR YOU!!! If you work with children, this book is for you and for them!

Think of this revealing book as a springboard or a catapult--often all that is needed to give you the boost that you need!

We all have our "Whys" in life:

These are questions that keep us awake at night, that make us spring from our beds early in the morning . . . queries that keep us on our toes, keep us guessing, searching, looking for answers and ways to impact others.

As I work with groups of students of all ages, I see the same resistance over and over again, and it puzzles me. In part, I believe this is because we get caught up in the system of mechanical and technical perfection in writing, and it steals our desire to produce free-flowing ideas. I want to throw a wrench in the system, bringing it all to a screeching halt!

Why do I feel this way? Or even care?

Because I cannot understand why we would avoid something that allows us to freely express ourselves. If it's worth writing, it's worth sharing; and if it's worth sharing, it's worth writing.

One of the most critical things we can give to our children (or ourselves) is the freedom to exercise the "Expression Muscle."

By encouraging creative writing, you are giving a beautiful gift to your children, or yourself, or to anyone: the Gift of finding that brilliant voice we all have!

In the following pages, you will find a Toolbox of ideas to help in your homes or classrooms or with your own personal writing.

This is a joyful journey to an amazing place, and I will happily be by your side as you build confidence in a crazy-fun way! I will encourage you to hang on and enjoy the ride, embrace expressing yourself, and opening yourself to moments of vulnerability and creativity. I deeply believe that by the end of this writing experience you will look back over all of the growth you've attained and see how joyful the journey was, and how far you've progressed.

Please remember to have fun, exercise your glorious Expression Muscle, and realize that it's easier than you think! You might just find you love it . . . you might even find that it's one of your new favorite things.

16

Three

Tips and Thoughts

Creative Writing is a Treasure! As we start "digging around," beautiful things will begin to surface. In the process of writing, hidden gems are just waiting to be found: diamonds, rubies, and precious gold will emerge and surely delight the writer and the reader!

As we begin "unearthing" these precious pieces, there are a few key tips to remember:

As parents and teachers, one of the most critical things we can give to our children is the freedom to exercise their "Expression Muscle." The gift of finding and using their unique voice is essential in life!

It is IMPERATIVE that we **Dump Perfectionism!** It is a beautiful thing to be Perfectly Imperfect in writing and in life. Teaching this to our kids and to ourselves as early as possible will only strengthen the desire to create from a place that feels right and whole and fulfilling.

Content is the most important ingredient in writing! While it is true that "Punctuation Saves Lives," it matters little if there is nothing written to save.

Throw out that dreaded Red Pen; in my opinion, it should be banished from ever sprinkling ink on the creative writing of others (especially children; we are here to encourage the creative process--not stifle it). There are ways of encouraging that don't "destroy" the art of another. Try using a sticky-note here and there, talk through ways of adding or deleting, help with the spelling, grab a thesaurus together and come up with new words to use--the list is endless! The point is to celebrate how amazing their effort and work are and to keep them growing!

Be careful and aware of not getting caught up in all the DOs and DON'Ts: this is creativity at its finest! There is a time and a place for all the rules, and this is not that time or place.

Look up definitions, not spellings: when your kiddos ask how to spell a word, go ahead and help them with the answer; when they ask what a word means, send them on a search! There is a huge difference in finding the definition and searching sometimes endlessly for a word they may never locate when they cannot spell it. A few key examples--ptarmigan, ubiquitous, icicles, inebriated, through and thorough, they're-their-there (use in sentences), onomatopoeia ...

Go ahead, just try looking one of these up for spelling; nothing more than a wild-goose chase coupled with tears of frustration when the search ends empty-handed.

Inspire Creativity: the best way to inspire is to model behavior for others to emulate; work alongside the children you teach and watch the magic happen! As you write, you could even "think out loud" about your process in a subtle, non-invasive way, giving guidance indirectly.

Writing is art expressed in words: we are working with artists--some in embryo--honor that!

Words have Power: Take the time to discuss the power of our words--how they can build and how they can tear down. Focus on the fact that even a negative topic can be handled proactively.

As we get to work, digging, we discover or unearth the **big questions**--the Roots of our story! This is where we ask the 6 Big Ones: *Who? What? When? Where? Why? How?* The answers to these questions serve to strengthen our plot and overall content.

In writing, we must uncover all the secrets of our story through **sensory images.** It's time to explore all of the details that allow us to fully "experience" the story through how it looks, sounds, feels, tastes and smells. These are the very things that will make a story viable and intrigue the reader and the writer.

Observation of the world around us is key. It is in these moments that we will likely stumble upon who our characters are; the details of our setting and environment will suddenly come to life before our eyes, and a story will begin to emerge. Building the perfect character(s) around what we observe is priceless. There is nothing quite like taking the time to visit places that delight you and your children: nature, old buildings, heavily populated areas, sanctuaries or wonders of the world . . . In these places, the most fascinating details of a story begin to develop in the imagination.

Writing requires embracing what comes: as we write, or as we teach writing, we should be aware that we may find a few buried feelings or emotions as we start digging and building and developing characters and their stories.

"So this, I believe, is the central question upon which all creative living hinges: Do you have the COURAGE to bring forth the treasures that are hidden within you?"

--Brene Brown

Writing doesn't always come easy, in fact, when working with kids, it can feel a lot like digging around in a compost pile in search of diamonds! Yes, a certain amount of wallowing will likely happen, but *hang out there long enough and the benefits will prove worthwhile*--as that soil reveals treasures, so will their abilities. Stand back and be amazed as those seeds and stories go from being planted to germinating to growing into a living thing that can THRIVE!

Creative Writing is a precious and deep Expression of the Soul . . . as *unfolding* as the petals of a flower. We do not fuss over the details; we appreciate the beauty.

-Stacey Lytle

21

Four

The Writer's Toolbox

Every job to be done requires a certain number of "tools," and writing is no exception. A carpenter's toolbox may look a bit different than a writer's toolbox, but they both serve the same purpose.

Our toolbox may not contain hammers, nails, or screwdrivers; it may not have blueprints, building materials, or pliers, either. Still, the tools for writing accomplish many of the same things. At times, we need a symbolic jack-hammer to break up our word clumps, drills that dig deeper for ideas and meaning, pick-axes that chip away unnecessary words or sections of writing, and perhaps sandpaper that will smooth out some rough edges. Bringing in the "heavy duty" equipment is often helpful as we start finding those gems that are hidden and sometimes stuffed deep inside! Digging takes hard work and dedication, and sometimes a little prodding and encouragement. There may be times when one of the most-used tools in your box will be a handy box of tissues--to wipe away the tears of frustration, or the tears of joy when something wonder-full comes from your heart and your story is told!

To begin, we need to throw open our snazzy Writer's Toolbox! Inside this box of treasures, we find: paper, sketch pads, pencils, watercolors, stationery, pens, sticky-notes, erasers, and maybe a bit of glitter and glue. Yes, I am a **paper-and-anything-crafty addict** . . . and proud of it! What I love is that you can personalize and customize this toolbox to perfectly fit *your* writing needs! Does that mean a type-writer, an organized stack of file-folders, or random notebooks filled with doodles and sketches of new characters and exciting story plots? It means *whatever you need it to mean* to write properly and comfortably.

In addition to the crafty things above, your Writing Toolbox should also be filled with some of the best basics; these are a few of my favorites:

Ideas--a.k.a. Writing Prompts:

I have you totally covered on the Writing Prompts--this book is loaded with some of the best and you can choose from any section, no matter your age or ability. These are simply a springboard to get your thoughts going, so play with them and see what inspiration comes from the experience!

Games:

Games are a fabulous way to reach and interact with kids--they won't even realize they are in the middle of learning because they'll be having such a blast playing! The idea is to get words spinning around in their heads, and there are multitudinous ways to do this; get creative and be sure to check out the chapter titled, "Games, Games, Games." In the meantime, a few of the essential items to grab for your Toolbox are: a set of dice, magnetic words or magnetic letters, the board-game "Scrabble," games like "Bananagrams," and "Appletters," a whiteboard and markers, and index cards that have various letters of the alphabet written on them.

Great Books:

This list could take a chapter or two all by itself! The main point is to surround yourself with the best books; books that inspire and delight . . . books that fill the mind with wonder . . . books that touch the heart and send you on a quest for the next one that hopefully tops the last because you can't wait to read more! The kinds of books you never want to put down!

Inspiration and A Comfortable Environment go hand-in-hand, in my opinion. The best moments of writing come when we are in a place that uplifts and strengthens us. Our most amazing pieces of writing will often not come from sitting at a desk (unless that is where you're most comfortable). Allow yourself or those you work with to find a comfy spot, bring on the throw-pillows, a soft blanket, pull out the chocolates or climb to a branch in your favorite tree or sprawl out under the clouds . . . These are the moments that our brains can let loose and be free to just create fantastic pieces of work. I have children who insist on hanging upside-down to do their work, or sit on top of the monkey-bars gazing out at the far-off sunset. . . whatever works for them, works for me!

Moments in nature and moments in crowded places . . .

I could have added this to the Inspiration-And-A-Comfortable-Environment section above, but the point is that we need to "get out" to get out of our heads! So often, we get stuck, we over-think, we struggle . . . All of the details of a story can freely flow to us when we put ourselves in new places and experience new feelings and surroundings. The moments of *Observation* where we work on all of the details of character and setting are priceless! Take yourself or your kiddos to outside areas and allow time to hear all of the delightful sounds; write about them. What do you hear? How do you feel when you hear these sounds? Are you filled with exhilaration, or does a gentle peace sweep over you just as the light breeze that floats past? What do you smell? Write about it. Help your reader feel like they are in that very spot.

When they read your words, does their mouth water or their nose perk up as you describe the scents? Take the time to observe people, structures, scenery--from these random things you may find your favorite characters or the setting of your next story. Pause, eyes closed, and just "feel." Is the sun warming you from the outside in? Is the rain pelting down and pushing you onward, or is a light mist covering your eye-glasses and dampening your skin? Is the wind brushing across your face and playing with the curls in your hair? Sensory Imagery is POWERFUL, so take advantage of it and have fun sharing what you experience!

If you are looking for some serious laughter in your life--spend a few minutes delving into the world of **Mad Libs!** The creativity may astound you as you play with adverbs, adjectives, nouns, verbs, etc. There is a plethora of ideas when working with parts of speech. My urging here is to have a *handy list of words* for your kids to pull from in each category required by the game. Also, be sure to check out a few games listed for you in the "Games, Games, Games" section of this book.

I've decided to add a bonus chapter at the end of the book with a few of my favorite lists that I have readily available for my children, and anyone else. So, be sure to check out "Lists, Lists, Lists," and share them freely to spark the use of some great words.

Vocabulary words that inspire! One of my preferred tools is the use of new, unexplored VOCABULARY words!!! Yes, I'm excited about this one! Why? Because I've seen delight in the eyes of children when they "know" words after we take the time to learn them, and then ... BAM! All of a sudden, those words show up *everywhere* they look! They appear on the pages of their books, on signs, in movies . . . it's a marvelous and empowering thing!

To ensure the most meaningful impact with new Vocabulary Words, please do not simply assign a list of words to kids to look up and define. This does not inspire and excite--this bores and frustrates because it is nothing more than tedious busy work. I believe in inspiring kids-- and an easy way is to quickly dig through books your students will be covering in the near future and pull out words that may be unfamiliar.

Each week, define them, write them on a white board, and challenge students to write the most ahhhh-mazing story possible using their new words. What does this do? For a start, students know exactly what that new word means, and after using it in a story that needs to be clear and coherent, the words are put into the right context. Second, that new vocabulary word is now a part of *their* vocabulary. They can freely own it because they've taken the time to fully understand and use it well. It has been my experience that when approaching vocabulary in this way, kids are filled with a natural curiosity and a willingness to perform on a higher level than they would by simply defining words.

Library Trips--or a well-stocked **Home Library.** Both are terrific!!! I have now adjusted to using our Home Library, and when needed, adding to it with additional purchases. Not only do I love having such a wide variety of literature at our fingertips, but I've found I no longer pay zillions of dollars each year in library fines and lost-book fees. Our trips to the library now are for a day of research, but no longer include carrying out bucket-loads of books that vanish all too quickly in our world!

Narration:

This isn't a tool to be used only for the younger students, although, it is ideal for those who are new to writing or struggle with the writing process. There are many, many times when our brains will go so much faster than our fingers. Narration just might be an answer to your prayers! If you have a student in your life that just can't get ideas out; if the tears flow faster than the words on the page; you might consider aiding them or finding a handy recording device into which they can narrate their stories and ideas. It is likely that their mouth can keep up with their brain more easily than any fingers are able. These recordings can then be transcribed at a later time. *Voilà!* Frustrations are limited and writing is magnified!

Dictation:

For young children, dictation is a valuable way for ideas and words to be stored for later writing or typing. Little hands can seldom write or type as quickly as the brain can create stories, or parts of stories, such as quotes, setting descriptions, character traits, and intriguing beginning lines or dramatic conclusions. A digital recorder, old tape-recorder, or even a willing parent with high-quality typing skills can document the workings of a writer's imagination before elements or details are forgotten. It's a way to put every literary creation into a cupboard where a writer can go to take out pieces--small or large--whenever they're ready to form their story. In the meantime, they can relax, knowing their other story-chunks and words are safe and remembered.

For adults, this is an equally crucial component. Adults are often distracted, although for different reasons, perhaps, and need a place to keep *their* ideas for later use.

The same tools are supportive, and even a notebook kept in the purse, pocket or backpack for jotting down thoughts is better than trusting that you "won't forget."

In many settings, educators have used the ritual of reciting words, sentences, or paragraphs that are then copied carefully by students. This tried and tested method has shown to serve as no more than an evaluation of the students' listening and penmanship skills. While it may be a traditional form of keeping students writing and learning to pay attention, there is a far better way that benefits the students and the teacher. We call this "Copy Work," and it does not masquerade as an effective method of narration or dictation.

Copy Work:

Copy Work is an innovative idea introduced by educator Charlotte Mason. While she may not have been the first, or the only person to use this tool and recognize its value, she certainly gave it new life. In summary, students learn spelling, penmanship, memorize worthwhile quotes, and learn to copy words from a piece of paper all in one exercise. While some people make a list on a page, I have found it much more effective to put quotes of various lengths and difficulty from a multitude of genres onto strips of paper. One strip of paper contains one quote-- from a book, from The Declaration of Independence, from scripture, from poetry, or any other source with messages worth sharing. The length of the quotes range from short sentences to one full paragraph. Only one strip of paper is drawn from a container, such as a "Copy Jar," daily. A Copy Book is purchased--it can be as simple as a ruled notebook or as fancy as a personally-decorated journal--and the quotes are dated and copied carefully just for the pleasure of it. While quotes need to be written with care, work is not evaluated, but rather stored so that the student can later see how their abilities have improved, and how interesting and enjoyable the quotes are to re-read. The only main rules are that genuine effort is made to keep the words on the lines of the page, so they do not become a size that exceeds them. Also, if a quote is drawn more than once in a year, it is put back in the jar and another is chosen. Quotes are typed by the parent, teacher or whoever is helping the student decorate the jar being used for quotes.

The bonus of this method is that it is an excellent tool for the mind, and adults also find it keeps their memories and recording skills sharp. A certain delight is found in each quote, and meaning is attached to an otherwise tedious venture.

And lastly, ***examples to follow and emulate*** . . . This is where you come into the picture if you are working with students, or if you are the one writing. It's time to look for those examples that serve to inspire you--those that are worth emulating! I cannot express this enough--*please* take the time to write *with* your kids/students! Have them share their work and you share yours, as well. What a powerful influence you will have! Give those kiddos in your life a remarkable example to follow and someone that motivates them to write. Modeling writing (and anything worthwhile, for that matter) is essential! There are many works available and the work you share may be exactly what will touch those in your sphere of influence.

Above, we covered some of the "Physical Tools" we need to accomplish our work. In addition, we have a few tools that bear explaining, *in spite of the fact that they are not often considered, these tools are equally crucial;* the tools that buoy us up when the going gets rough, when the doubts crowd in, and when our brains are stuck and all the creativity seems to have vanished. Let's call these our "Emotional Tools."

The **"Emotional Tools"** are essential! Why? Because writing is focused business! It's the amazing business of self-expression, and we sometimes get caught up in the ideas--or the lack of ideas--and need a little nudge to get moving.

There will be times when the best thing we can offer to ourselves is a "Rocket Thought." During those moments of needing to get moving, we can give ourselves that necessary lift-off by simply saying in our minds:

"5...

4...

3...

2...

1...

Get to it!!!"

Brainstorm and free-write! No more sitting and over-thinking!

Grab a piece of chocolate for an extra little boost and Get Writing--start with anything! Get creating--let any idea be a "springboard," and get off the spot that is holding you back. Just move the words along until they flow!

The emotional tools we need are **Self-Belief** (your story is worth telling!), **Desire** (if that dream is in you, it is just waiting for you to share it . . .), and **Dancing With Your Fears!** (Fear holds us back from far too many opportunities, but it is real. If you need to, pretend nobody will read your writing but you; you can also imagine your target audience loving what you've written! Do not ever allow fear of any kind to control you or hold you back from the things your heart desires to express. Decide to embrace the situation as it is and move forward with the dance!)

Writing isn't saved for those with Special Talent or only those who are publishing or making huge impacts obvious to the world; writing is for Everyone! Writing is truly a gift we give to ourselves or to those we work with or mentor. It has been my experience that many feel overwhelmed, fearful, or burdened, and wish there could be a way to save them from the process completely. While there's no fool-proof magic to make writing effortless--no short-cuts or easy ways out--there is a Perfect Toolbox for you, and it is loaded with all of the tools a person needs to start to write, or, to improve their writing skills, and help others to do the same. Creative Writing should be held in a sacred place when working with kids . . . or anyone else.

The World of Creative Writing is a singular place where we don't have to follow all of the rules; it is a place where we don't have to worry about the spelling and grammar and punctuation. A place where we simply concentrate on developing characters that are engaging; settings that make us and others feel they are present in the story along with the characters; plots and conflicts and endings that keep us riveted and holding our breath as we turn each page. In essence, Creative Writing is a journey of the heart making its way through one magnificent experience after another. These moments involve opening ourselves to feel and be vulnerable, spill the very things we are made of onto pages that may one day change a life--of someone else, or the writer, or both.

After all of the creating is complete, we polish our work with punctuation, spelling-checks, and common-sense editing . . . After all, once a gorgeous painting has been completed, we frame it.

While you don't need numerous resources for editing, there are stacks of books with helps for everything from where to put your commas and apostrophes to spelling five-syllable words.

I urge you to go to your local library and/or bookstore, and look through these editing sources to find one or two that best fit your needs. Be sure they are a comfortable fit for you, or they will gather dust on the shelf like Great-Aunt Mable's hand-me-down knick-knacks. Most of these books are also sold in a variety of places online, so find the best price once you've made your choice and utilize those guides over and over again. Who knows? They might become your new family heirlooms.

Here are a couple of suggestions to start you on your search:

There, Their, They're: A No-Tears Guide to Grammar from the Word Nerd by Annette Lyon

Eats, Shoots & Leaves: The Zero Tolerance Approach to Punctuation by Lynne Truss

Happy Writing!!!

Five

Wee Littles

What a beautiful time to discover the amazing world that exists in your children--The World of Creative Writing! A world where anywhere your imagination travels is perfect, wanted, and magical.

Remember, it is never too early or too late to jump into the world of creativity . . . what a gift you are giving to the children you work with!

When working with Wee Littles--often those that are new to writing or those who may even be too little for writing on their own--NEVER FEAR!!! They are often some of the very best story-tellers! Creativity flows through them effortlessly and they are unafraid of sharing and rarely find the need to hold back. Their stories come together almost instantly!

To get started, simply give these sweet little people a sheet of drawing paper, crayons, colored pencils, or a brush and watercolors; set their ideas free as you read two or three writing prompts to them, and then guide them along. Some may wish to close their eyes as you read the prompt, allowing them to visualize their story. Have them begin by drawing whatever they feel inspired to draw, whether it has to do with the prompt or not. Encourage them to add as much detail as possible while drawing or coloring by asking them about their work (i.e. "What is this?" "What does he do?" "Will you draw that to show me?"). When they have developed a story, allow them to narrate to you uninterrupted. As the educator/parent, you may either record, type, or write as they speak. You may need to ask questions to keep the story going and to pull out additional details.

It is highly recommended that you put together a binder with plastic sleeves to keep these stories in as they will undoubtedly become priceless treasures! Hint: Have your kiddos design a cover for their binders and make sure to have them include their name as AUTHOR and ILLUS-TRATOR!!! If they choose to use words instead of pictures, that is just fine--they just need the chance to express themselves in whatever way they feel most comfortable and safe.

Now Let's Get Started!

1. "All of a sudden, while we were in the middle of the lake, our boat started leaking.!! Eeeeek! You won't believe what happened next . . ."

2. Describe just the right way to brush and floss your teeth--be sure to include every step! :)

3. Today is ICE CREAM INVENTION DAY!!! Wahoooooo! What flavors would you combine to make the latest and greatest ice cream creation? What would you name it? Who is the first person you'd share it with?

4. If you were an explorer, where would you explore? What would you find? Would you make a NEW Discovery? What foods do you take with you and what new foods do you try on your expedition?

5. It's Sandwich-Making Time! Yum!!! Make a list of your favorite ingredients! Then describe how your mouth feels after chomping down on that perfect first bite.

6. You've always dreamed of flying . . . TODAY is THE DAY!!! Would you rather fly on an airplane, a hot air balloon, a helicopter, on the wings of an eagle, or strapped on the back of a Pterodactyl? What does the world below you look like? Are things smaller or larger than you'd imagined? How does the air feel to you up so high?

7. "Once upon a time, there was a bear who woke up way too early from his winter hibernation. He walked to the entrance of his cave, stretched and _____"

8. What is the happiest moment you can remember in your whole entire life? How did you feel inside? What was happening? Who was with you?

9. Lucky YOU!!! You've just been asked to help build the world's largest and greatest playground! What things do you add in? Is there anything you'd leave out? Do you build it indoors or outside? Describe what it looks like when it is complete.

10. Yippeeeee!!! You finally made it to the front of the line--what a long wait! When you stepped up to order your double-cheeseburger, fries, and a chocolate shake, you were greeted by a very peculiar person who stopped you before you could even place your order. You were informed that THIS was the line to receive your Super Power!!! You screeched out a crazy-excited "Woo-hooooo!" and then asked for your Super Power . . . What did you ask for? How did you use it? What special things happen because of your new Super Power???

11. There is a giant wall in the big city near your home, and YOU get to paint it any way you'd like! What colors do you use? Do you add pictures or designs or both? Do you do it alone or invite others to join in on the fun?

12. If you had three wishes, what would you wish for?

13. Would you rather have no teeth--or no hair? Why? Which do you think would be the hardest to deal with, and why?

14. What is your favorite thing in the whole world to drink? How does it taste to you? How does it feel in your mouth? In your belly? Does it make you smile while you drink it?

15. What would you do if your dog really did eat your home

work? What if nobody believes you?

16. If an alien spaceship landed in your backyard and invited you aboard, would you go? If yes, what would you see inside? Would you fly anywhere? If not, what would you say, and then what would happen?

17. If you had $5,000 to spend, what would be the first thing you'd spend it on? Why?

18. Would you rather be trapped in a room with a bucket of buzzing mosquitoes, or with a hungry crocodile? Why?

19. It's pouring rain outside . . . You have to decide if the raindrops come down as jaw-breakers, cotton-candy, or Jolly Ranchers. What happens when the storm hits? Do others like your choice? Are you happy with your choice?

20. What would you do if you found a wallet filled with money on the street? Why?

21. "I never imagined that when I grew up I'd live next door to a fire-breathing dragon, a two-headed monster, and an ugly toad . . . These are some of the things I see when I look out my back widow, but also _____"

22. You just found a brand new planet--what an exhilarating day!!! You will be famous for sure! What do you call your new planet? Does life exist here? How much do you weigh on this planet? How does it feel to be the discoverer of such an amazing thing?

23. "My very favorite thing to do is _____. When I do this, I feel _____!"

24. "The funniest thing I ever saw was _____!"

25. Would you rather be really tall, or really short? Why?

26. Bath Time!!! But today is not your ordinary kind of bath day. Today, you get to choose between soaking in a tub of icy lemonade, or a tub of tomato soup. Which do you choose? And do you ask for a straw, or a spoon with that bath?

27. What really excites me is _____! When I think about it, I feel _____.

28. "My idea of the best teacher in the world is _____. He or she would let us do _____, and they would never ask us to do _____!"

29. Write a story about a singer who cannot stop singing, ever. All they do is sing and sing and sing. What is life like for them? How would you feel if singing was part of every-thing you ever did? Taking a shower, eating your cereal for breakfast, and even digging in the dirt would all be done while singing. Would this be okay with you, or would you wish for it to go away? Why?

30. If you could throw a giant party for everyone you know, what would you do? How would you decorate? Where would you hold the party? How many people would be there? Would you invite a clown?

Six

Littles

First things first: Pull out all of the Art Goodies-- sketch pads, pencils, watercolors, markers, colored pencils, crayons, and maybe even a bottle of glue and glitter to sparkle it up!!!

This group is a blast to work with! Their creative juices get flowing in a fabulous way! There may be some who are reluctant to begin writing and may need some assistance--remember this is all about fostering a love of writing. Please don't get hung-up--or allow your students to get-hung up--on the mechanics and the "rights" and "wrongs" of writing. This is a time to have fun, to use imaginations, to dig in and look for words they don't necessarily use on a regular basis, to bring to life a story of their own dreaming, and to find the diamonds in their writing. As a facilitator, one of the best things you can do for them is to stand by, ready and willing, to encourage ideas--whatever they may be, or to help with the spelling of words that stump them and hold them back. Be willing to help and possibly even guide by asking additional questions when they seem "stuck."

Allow them to work on a visual prior to the creation of their story; music is often a nice touch as they work with their writing prompts. Encourage your kiddos to head outdoors for a little fresh air when writing--this often opens their eyes to all sorts of new possibilities for their story.

One of our all-time-favorite things to do at the completion is to have a "Readers' Theater." Organize a time for your students to share their stories and illustrations with others. Finally, be sure to have a special portfolio book to keep these treasures in! An easy idea is a simple binder with a front sleeve (great for a cover page--be sure to have them make it and add their names as the AUTHOR and ILLUSTRATOR!), add in a few plastic sleeves for their stories and illustrations, and they've got a fabulous start to their very own book!

Ready, Set, Go!!!

1. What is your favorite sound? When you hear it how do you feel inside?

2. If you were an alien what color would you be? How many eyes would you have? Would you have a tail? What size would you be? What would your alien-superpower be?

3. Imagine you are a baby bird; it is a beautiful spring day . . . today is THE DAY to learn how to FLY!!! What happens?

4. What is your favorite thing on your face? Is it your nose? Your eyes? How about your smile? Is it the way your eyes wink? The way your dimples dimple? The cute freckles across your sweet nose?

5. What is the absolute scariest, most terrifying thing about being an ant? What is it like to be that small? Or do you love being an ant? Why?

6. What are three things you wish you could do?

7. Wow! Life without erasers . . . what is that like?

8. What is your dream pet? What do you do with your pet and how does it change life as you now know it?

9. "Once upon a time, there was a cowboy who was terrified of cows . . ."

10. What is the bravest, most courageous thing you've ever done?

11. If you had a million dollars, what would you do first? How would you spend all your money?

12. You just came upon an old antique key . . . what lock does it open? When you finally unlock it, what do you find inside?

13. It's your lucky day! You have just been handed an assortment of paint brushes and all the paint supplies you could dream of! You get to paint your house or your bedroom any color you want! What does that look like? Remember, you can choose any colors and any designs! Describe in detail how amazing it will look when you're finished!

14. YOU are a FAMOUS CHEF!!! What is on your menu and who do you serve?

15. What is the hardest thing you've ever had to wait for? What was it like for you? How did you help pass the time while you waited?

16. "At the end of the rainbow, I saw the most brilliant _____!"

17. You are headed to a deserted island for an entire year . . . you chose to be here and you are crazy-excited for what is ahead of you! You get to take one person with you. Who do you choose, and why? Write about all of the adventures you have, then write about your favorites.

18. Why are rules and laws important? Which do you think are the most important? Why?

19. Would you like to be famous? Why or why not? What does "fame" look like to you? Does being famous change who you are and how you live your life, or do you and your life remain the same?

20. "In the abandoned home, tucked away in the far corner, sat an unusual-looking trunk. My curiosity got the best of me and I found myself jetting across the room . . . I gently lifted the lid and _____!"

21. Oh, my goodness!!! All the electricity is GONE! You save the day, you save your city, YOU are a hero! What does this day look and feel like? Do you see yourself as a hero? How does it feel to come up with the solution to bring electricity back to everyone around you?

22. Please sit down and tell me how the elephant got its wrinkles!

23. In your opinion, what is the most important job in the world? Why is it so important?

24. Yippeeee!!! YOU get to create a NEW HOLIDAY! What is it? What or who does it celebrate? What fun things happen on your holiday? What day of the year is your holiday?

25. You are a migratory bird--time to fly south for the winter! While all your bird friends were getting ready to go, you were distracted and missed take-off time. What distracted you? How did you feel when you realized all the others had flown south and you had been left behind? What happens over the winter? What do you do? Who do you meet? What adventures await?

26. And just like that--YOU became a GIANT! How tall are you? Who is your closest friend? What adventures do you go on? Do you enjoy life as a giant?

27. You have one day to transform two people into animals. Whom do you choose and which animal (or animals) do you turn them into? Why did you choose them and how do you transform them from humans to animals? Are you happy

with the changes?

28. The Fortune Cookie Factory in China desperately needs your help writing new fortunes for their cookies to be shipped all over the world. What are the top ten "fortunes" you write to share with cookie eaters?

29. You are on a stage and YOU are the expert in all things regarding animals. The audience is anxiously waiting for you to explain a few things! Here's the start of your list: why raccoons have masks, why sea otters hold hands when they sleep, how butterflies taste with their feet, and if it's true that seahorses actually hold tails as they travel . . . How do you answer these questions, and what other fascinating things do you share?

30. What kind of weather best describes you? Sunshine, rain, snow, thunder, wind . . . Describe you and then choose a weather for the way your home feels. Why did you choose the type of weather you chose?

Seven

Middles

During this time of life, it is imperative that our students have an outlet to express themselves! The act of expressing oneself creates confidence and clarity, which is essential as these years often challenge who we think we are and who we believe we need to become.

I would recommend offering an "artistic" element to their writing at these ages as well. Art, in the form of writing or on a canvas, can be therapeutic and inspiring. Often times, one may surprisingly speak volumes above the other. The magic of offering both is that you will likely touch hearts and inspire greatness! So, pull out all the best stuff--the nice sketch pads, pastels, oil colors, water colors, or sketching pencils--then stand back, give them space, be available if they need you, and prepare to be amazed as you read them the writing prompts and they create! There is no "wrong" way to do it!

So... What Are You Waiting For? Let's Write a Little Magic!!!

1. You crack open your fortune cookie. Inside it reads, "Today might just be the best day of your life." You smile and the adventure begins . . . How did your adventure turn out? What was the best part?

2. Introduce your family . . . What events/times have made you closer as a family? What are two of your favorite memories as a family? What were you doing? Were you at home? Outside? On vacation? In the mountains?

3. Visualize a time when someone you love was laughing so hard they snorted! What happened to everyone around you? How did you react?

4. You've just been elected President of the United States of America! Time to prepare your inauguration speech! What do you share, what is most important to you? How do you plan to make the world a better place?

5. What is your favorite place in your house? Describe how it feels, smells, and looks. Is it peaceful, or crazy? What do you do there? Why is it your favorite? What is in this place? Is there furniture? A tree swing? A comfortable chair? What colors surround you?

6. You are walking down a cobblestone path and right in front of you is the shiniest penny you've ever seen! You bend down, pick it up, turn it from side to side, smile to

yourself--and just as you begin to stand back up . . . an endearing voice chimes in, "Find a penny, pick it up, all day long you'll have good luck!" You look all around to see where the voice was coming from and you see _____ .

7. How do you know when someone loves you? How does it make you feel? Do they always have to say, "I love you," for you to know? Write about a time that you felt loved or a time that you showed love to another person.

8. What is the hardest thing about being your age? What is expected of you? What expectations do you place on yourself?

9. Your new friend just delivered a beautifully wrapped-- but interesting--gift of bacon ice cream and garlic-flavored bubblegum. How do you say "Thank you," in a letter?

10. And then there was the day that your worst enemy turned into an animal . . . How did that turn out?

11. Do you have a favorite memory from when you were just five or six years old? Who was there? What was happening? Close your eyes if you are struggling to recall the details and look around . . . What do you see? Write all about it!

12. You were just made Ruler of the World!!! What laws do you get rid of? What great things do you make happen? How is life changed for you and for others? Is it better? Are you pleased with the impact you've made?

13. What happens when an elephant eats too much? Should you run? Should you hide? Or maybe grab your camera . . . or a snow shovel . . .

14. The tragic story of a lemonade stand: "The day started out just as I had planned, but then_____. I just couldn't believe it!"

15. It's time for a Safari!!! You are headed to Africa for the summer! Woo-hoo!!! How do you prepare for this adventure?

16. "Just as I was cleaning up the leftover pieces of sidewalk-chalk, I glanced back over my shoulder and caught a last glimpse of the artwork we'd created that day. I knew the storm was about to hit and those creations would be washed away with the rain ... Next, what I saw shocked and amazed me! Those sidewalk chalk creations now stood-up right before me! I _____ "

17. Has something ever upset or hurt you and you just wanted to keep it all in? Did it help to keep it in? Do you think it might be helpful to let it out? Is there someone in your world that you trust enough to share these hurts with? If you're still holding on to these, try writing them down and letting them go.

18. You've just discovered a tremendously special gift-- YOU are able to communicate with animals! What is your first thought when you discover this new "gift"? What do you do with it?

19. You get to be the Teacher for a day! What do you teach, and how do you teach it? What is your favorite kind of student? What do you do to make sure your students all feel special at the end of the day? Would you go back and do it again or would you rather only be a student?

20. Peer Pressure--ugh!!! Write about a time you were talked into doing something you really didn't want any part of. How did you turn this situation into a positive thing for your future? Or write about a time that you didn't fall into the ugly trap of Peer Pressure . . . What did it feel like to stand firm? Was it hard, or lonely, or was it wonderful and rewarding? Did you help others by being a strong example?

Did you help yourself?

21. You are in charge of planning the next big vacation. You've just been told you can plan to visit ANYWHERE you've ever dreamed of! Wow! What do you plan? Where will you go? What will you see? Who will be joining you for this vacation? Do you fly, go by ship, drive, or maybe ride horseback to your destination?

22. What is a "Hero"? Do you know any heroes? Do you live with a hero? What qualities make a person heroic? Is there someone you wish to be just like when you are older that you believe is a hero?

23. Choose one person you'd like to spend an entire day with. What do you do? What do you talk about? Are there questions you'd like to ask of this person? How do you feel at the end of the day? Do you wish the day would never end?

24. "Life is like a box of chocolates," "Life is like a Roller Coaster," "Life is like a bowl of cherries . . ." What do all of these quotes mean to you? Do you agree with them or disagree? Why is life like a box of chocolates or a roller coaster or a bowl of cherries?

25. It's time to choose your favorite car . . . The Car Lot is OPEN! Time to test drive! What do you choose? What is the year, make, and model? How about the color? Is it a convertible? Is it lifted? Does it seat 2 or 20? Where do you go? What sights do you see? What speeds did you reach? Did you obey the traffic signs? Who saw you driving? Did they run, or wave and smile? Who was lucky enough to be in the passenger seat? Do you find a way to buy this car or was it a dream-day of playing?

26. What annoys or irritates you the very most? What hap-

pens on the inside of you when you feel irritated? Do you sometimes feel like you might explode? If so, how do you control it? Do you think of something else? Do you walk away? Do you turn it into a joke? What is your secret???

27. What is worth standing in a massively long line??? Choose just one thing ... what is it? Why is it worth waiting for? How long would you wait? While you are in line, what could you do to pass the time more joyfully?

28. Think of one person (or two) that has made your life better? Write to them; let them know the difference they've made for you. What example have they given to you that you want to share with others? Do they make you wish to be a better person? Write about them here and take a few minutes to send a letter their way! YOU will be making a difference in their lives!

29. Today is your lucky day! The State Fair is in town and you just heard the announcement that they are handing out SUPER POWERS to the first 25 people through the gates. You jump on your bike and make it!!! What you see before you are five separate kiosks to choose from ... This is where the SUPER POWERS are divvied out! Did you get in the right line? What SUPER POWER did you receive? What do you do with it?

30. "How happy did you DECIDE to be today?" Do you believe happiness is a choice? Do you believe you have the ability to DECIDE how today looks for you? Do you believe you get to choose--that you get to shape the day--that you get to make it extraordinary? Is it possible that these things are all true and that the day doesn't get to shape you? Write your thoughts ...

Eight

Biggles

What the heck is a "Biggle"? Ya know, the children that started out as "Wee Littles" and "Littles," flew right past the "Middles," and before you blinked they stood before you as your Biggles! These are the big kids that may very well tower over you, but still look to you for your help and your guidance.

The following writing prompts are for that fabulous group of not-so-little-kids!

If you are looking for Crazy-Amazing results--join them! Grab a notebook and pen and start writing alongside them--you may be the very inspiration they need most! Dig deep--those diamonds are waiting. They may be found in moments of vulnerability, moments of creativity, or moments that are filled with dreams just waiting to become realities!

I'd suggest choosing one writing prompt per week: write it, put it down for a bit, ponder on it, come back to it, add, take away, keep digging and then share together! Discuss, learn about each other, and undoubtedly, about yourself...

Whatever happens, it's bound to be extaordinary!!!

Ready For the Magic???

1. Do you wish you could return to a moment in your past? Why? Would you change anything? What did this time mean to you?

2. When in your life have you been a leader? What did you learn about leadership? About yourself? Is this a comfortable place for you, or would you rather be tucked "behind the scenes"?

3. You are a Talk Show Host!!! Whom do you wish to interview? What questions are you dying to know about this person? What surprises come from your time with them?

4. Comfort Foods . . . ahhhh! What is your "go-to" during crummy moments? Describe that first bite . . . what did it taste like? How did your body react? Did you experience "comfort" with this magical food?

5. You're sitting in the grandstands when a set of keys drop into your lap. These are not just any keys--they are the keys that fire up the NASCAR that is waiting on the track right in front of you. The crowd starts cheering you on . . . they are waiting . . . you stand and _____!

6. You have the opportunity to design the perfect "hang-out" spot. What does it include? It is indoors, outdoors, or both? What events/attractions are present? Describe "Opening Day"!

7. You are witness to a mean act against another. What do you do? How do you make a difference--by doing something, or by making sure you behave in a kind way in your

life that is better than the people you see that are mean?

8. Choose two to three songs that perfectly describe you and your life; it's as if they were written for you! Do you need to add another verse or two? Go for it--make these songs yours!

9. "When you're pinned against the wall, and the only option is to overcome, a miracle takes place! It is in that very moment that you learn just how strong you are and what you are capable of!" What are your strategies for dealing with challenging times and turning them into victories?

10. Which country fascinates you? At which season would you most like to visit? What would be the top things you'd need to experience there? NO limits--what would you REALLY do? How long would your visit last?

11. What will you do as a parent? What will you do differently from your parents when raising your own children? What might you do just the same? What is the biggest gift you received from being raised in your home? Will you pass that on?

12. Do you believe there is life on other planets? How do you imagine it looks? How does it behave? Do they possess the same emotions and process thoughts as we do? Do they live in families? Are they more or less self-sufficient as a people? What are their resources?

13. "Those who don't jump will never fly." Is this a truth or a non-truth in your eyes? What thoughts does this stir within you?

14. You have a Fairy Godmother/Godfather who comes to you in your greatest hour of despair . . . What do you ask of her/him?

15. Adventure Time! These four things are on your list for the upcoming week: Deep-Sea Diving, Cliff-Climbing, Hang-Gliding, and Standing on a Stage in front of thousands . . . Which delights you? Which terrifies you? What comes of this adventurous week?

16. Describe your highest moment in life; who was with you? What were you doing? How did it feel? Do you wish you could go back to this place and time?

17. Now describe your lowest moment in life; who was there to lift you? How did you move past this? How has this experience strengthened you? What did you learn about yourself?

18. It started out as any ordinary Tuesday would. You woke, began your day, and then, OUT OF NOWHERE _____

19. Introduce your family. What events/times have made you closer as a family? From whom have you learned the most? Recall a favorite memory or two with your family and write every detail. Close your eyes to help you visualize those things that may have faded in your memories.

20. What is courage? Who possesses it? Share a time when you were courageous or wished you had been able to exercise more courage.

21. You are in charge of creating the messages for the Candy Valentine Hearts this year! What would you change? What sayings would you add in an instant? Which would be banished forever?

22. You get to bring one Game/Board Game to life. Which would you choose, and why? Now go live it . . . what happens? Who do you invite to join you in your game of life?

23. What does the perfect day look like to you? Where are you? What are you doing? What are you wearing? Are you alone, in a crowd of strangers, with your family, or hanging out with your "bestie"?

24. Have you ever known someone who has "EVERY-THING"? What was that like for you? If you look a little closer, do they really have everything? What does that even mean?

25. What would you invent that could make the world a better place to be? Who does it help? Do you bring others along to help you in your invention? Does this spur new creative ideas to continue inventing?

26. Is there anything worth risking your life for? If so, what? And why?

27. Write about your greatest friendship. What have you learned? Is there anything you would "rewind" and try again?

28. Your body has just taken flight into the most spectacular dive you've ever performed. Just as you are about to make contact with the water beneath you, you notice something that takes your breath away . . . it's _____

29. Today, take the time to write a letter to someone. Who has touched you? Who has pushed you to be the best YOU can be? Who deserves to hear what a gift they've been to your life?

30. You are mid-mountain, pack on your back, sweat seeping from your pores, ready to give up, ready to give in, pushed beyond your limits . . . What do you do? Whom do you call of for help? How do you find the inner-strength and belief in yourself to keep going? Who is your greatest

support? These are the people to surround yourself with in all times and in all places. Write about them and when you find yourself in those moments in life, call on them, go to them; don't do it alone--we are better together!

Nine

Games, Games, Games!!!

If you or your students are feeling "Stuck," or just need to liven things up--throw out the normal routine and dig into some game-time fun!

Index Cards are a fantastic resource for your toolbox of games:

Grab 26 index cards and write a letter of the alphabet on each A-Z. Draw from the pile and name all of the words that come to mind that begin with that letter. You can set a reasonable time limit to make it more challenging for those with quicker skills (for example: name every word starting with the letter "a" in two minutes . . .). Choose five words and create a fun story with them!

Alphabet Animals is another fun category to get you thinking: Start with the letter "a," or grab from your stack of index cards if you wish. This was a favorite in our home when our children were young. Play a game naming off all of the animals that begin with that letter; draw pictures, tell stories, and for little ones, allow them to narrate to you. This can actually be done with any age group.

Need a few ideas for animals?

A – aardvark, alligator, armadillo

B – buffalo, badger, bald eagle

C – camel, cheetah, caribou

D – diamondback rattlesnake, deer mouse, duck

E – eagle, elephant, emu

F - flamingo, falcon, fox

G – gecko, gorilla, gazelle

H – hippopotamus, hyena, harbor seal

I – iguana, ibex, impala

J – jaguar, jackrabbit, jackal

K – koala bear, kangaroo, killer Whale

L – llama, lemur, leopard

M – manatee, meerkat, macaw

N – narwhal, Nubian bee-eater, num bat

O – octopus, orangutan, opossum

P – penguin, porcupine, peacock

Q – quail, quoll, quokka

R – reindeer, raccoon, red howler monkey

S – sea turtle, shrew, sloth

T – turkey, Tasmanian devil, tortoise

U – urchin, urial, uakari

V – vulture, vicuna, viper

W – warthog, woodchuck, wallaby

X – xenops, xerus, x-ray tetra

Y – yak, yellow baboon, yellow-rumped siskin

Z – zebra, zebu, zorilla

Memory Match

Memory-style matching games are easy to make and fun to use. To make a game like this, you can make a set of matching cards using index cards. Simply write each capital letter on one card and its lower-case counterpart on another card. Turn all the cards over and arrange them on a desk. Students must find both the capital and lower-case letter to make a match. Or, make the game more challenging for your students and add a vocabulary element. Have students match an alphabet letter to a picture that starts with that letter. Take it another step and work on synonyms and antonyms or present tense and past tense versions of words starting with those letters. So many ideas when working with memory matching--have fun!

Hangman

Hello spelling and vocabulary!

I love to use "Hangman" when introducing new topics that we are going to study in class, or clues for fun things coming up. I also like Hangman as a way to practice countries, states, capitals, anything! Choose a topic to work with and go for it. Need to work on prepositions or a review of vocabulary? Here you go!

Bean Bag Games

Do you want to get your children moving while you review letters of the alphabet? Write the 26 letters of the alphabet in random order on a plain shower curtain, and lay it out on the floor. Have bean bags ready to toss! Take turns tossing the bag, and as the bag lands near a letter, have the students shout out a word that begins with that letter. As they progress, step it up! Ask for adjectives or adverbs that begin with that letter ... or, have them toss three bags and come up with sentences using words that begin with the letters they landed on.

R & R – Repetition and Rhyme

Great for the Wee Littles and Littles in your life!

Repetition makes books predictable, and young readers love knowing what comes next. Start by gathering a few books with repeated phrases such as: *Alexander and the Terrible, Horrible, No Good, Very Bad Day* by Judith Viorst; *Brown Bear, Brown Bear, What Do You See?* by Bill Martin, Jr.; *Horton Hatches the Egg* by Dr. Seuss; and *The Little Engine That Could* by Watty Piper.

Also, throw in a few short, rhyming poems or stories. For example, read:

(Wolf voice:) "Little pig, little pig, let me come in."

(Little pig:) "Not by the hair on my chinny-chin-chin."

(Wolf voice:) "Then I'll huff, and I'll puff, and I'll blow your house in!"

After the wolf has blown down the first pig's house, your child will soon join in! Pause and give him or her a chance to fill in the blanks and phrases. Encourage these little ones to pretend to read, especially books that contain repetition and rhyme. Most children who enjoy reading will eventually memorize all or parts of a book and imitate your reading. This is a normal part of reading development, including mistakes made while pronouncing or "reading" words.

When children anticipate what's coming next in a story or poem, they have a sense of mastery over books, and also develop a relationship with them that helps them feel comfortable. When children feel power, they have the courage to try.

Around the World

UP for a little friendly competition?

This works best with a set or sets of flashcards. These cards can be math, vocabulary, spelling, geography . . . try states and capitals, countries of the world, etc.

Have all your students stand up, with the first student standing next to the student behind them, and so on in a line. You show a flashcard, and whoever is the fastest to say the correct answer moves on, like a relay. For a bonus, if a student makes it all the way around the room then they get to go against the teacher.

I Spy

Great For Teaching Nouns

Find an item to "spy," and then give clues like: "I spy something green (plant), or I spy something moving (clock)." Kids guess the noun you described. Simple!

I'm Thinking of Someone Who

(or of a Place That--) for teaching Proper Nouns

You can describe kids that are wearing certain clothing or give physical-appearance clues (like someone with a headband, or someone with fun freckles). You could describe them using things you know about them (like the fact that they like to play hockey or read books). You could also expand this to include well-known historical characters such as George Washington or Christopher Columbus by describing facts many people already know about them. Famous or not, your clues might be, "I'm thinking of someone (in our classroom or famous) who wears glasses/was the first president/loves to play soccer/sailed the ocean blue . . ."

Charades

Want to teach all about verbs?

Here you go--works like a charm!

To play this game, use a small whiteboard or index cards to show your acting volunteer clues for the verb the child is going to act out. I strongly suggest using verbs that are more interesting than just "run" or "hop," because these are great for beginners or to get the ball rolling, but more complex verbs give maximum benefit and fun! For example, how fun would it be to have the kids read a card and act out making a pizza, mixing a cake, cutting an onion, lifting weights, mowing the lawn, or building a fire? The ideas are endless, which is a good thing, because with the right "tools" their *desire* to play along may well seem endless!

Clues, Clues, Clues

Fun with Adjectives!

Have everyone sit in a circle, "criss-cross-apple-sauce," sitting close enough for knees to almost touch, but leaving enough space in the center for one child to sit. Have a bag filled with some of the craziest, most unusual items you can find. Choose someone to be "It," and the person who is "It" sits in the middle of the circle. Pull an item out of the bag; the job of the person who is "It," is to describe the item using five different adjectives. They will be racing against the circle! As soon as the item is pulled from the bag, toss a beanbag to one of the kiddos in the circle and let them compete with their own five adjectives. Who will be first to finish? The beanbag making its way around the circle or the person who is in the center shouting out five Awesome Adjectives??? If you are doing this with only one or two children, set a timer or a buzzer to add to the excitement for them to race against each other--and time!

How Would You . . . ?

Acting With Adverbs!

You will need one child at a time to be your actor with the rest of the class guessing which adverb they might be acting out. This can also easily be done one-on-one, or with a smaller group. Simply read out the scenario and the child can choose an adverb to act out.

"How would you act if you were sneaking out of the kitchen with a cookie?" They can then act out what comes to them, perhaps quietly or sneakily. Have the other kid--or yourself--guess what the adverb might be.

"How would you yell if a rattlesnake was near you (loudly)?" Or, "How would you move if you were a turtle (slow-ly)?" Have fun with this one, and add a possible bonus to the kids to come up with a few ideas of their own to act out!

Get Moving With Prepositions!

This one can be done with a group of any size. Simply call out a prepositional-type direction to tell them where to go. For example, "by the table," "on the rug," "near the bookcase," "under the table," etc. After playing a few rounds, have different kids call out the prepositions and play along with them!

What Would You Say . . .?

Playing with Interjections!

For this game, I give the kids different scenarios and ask them which interjection they would use in that situation. If they need some ideas for interjections, run over a fun list with them before starting: "Whew!" "Uh-oh!" "Ugh!" "Yay!" "Yippeeee!" "Good Grief!" "Yowza!" "Shoot!" "Oh, dear!" "Wow!" "Ouch!"

An example scenario: "What would you say if the top scoop of ice cream just fell from your ice-cream cone and splattered all over your brand-new shoes?" "Grrr," "Ugh!" and "Oh, brother . . ." and so on, would work well. "What would you say if a raging bull were charging your direction and you chose to wear your bright red shirt that day?" This is another game that is good for motivating the kids to come up with the scenarios. Join in on the fun, or sit back and be entertained by their creativity!

P.S. I love you!

Something important happens when children receive and write letters. They realize that the printed word has a purpose, and it becomes meaningful to them.

Send your child little notes; leave them on a pillow, send them in the mail, stick them in a lunch box, or start a little journal between the two of you. I've done this with my kids and it is a treasure! A couple of possible titles for the front cover of a writing journal could be: "Mom and Me," or "P.S. I love you!"

Pen-pals (though not utilized as they once were) are a fantastic way to teach our kids correspondence. You might consider taking the time to share the value of Thank-You letters or cards; a seemingly lost art that touches hearts.

Language is speaking, listening, reading, and writing. Each element supports and enriches every other element. Sending letters will help children become better writers, and writing will make them better readers, for example.

Flying Beach Balls

Small beach balls are a must in your Writing Toolbox! There are countless games to use these for! One of my favorites is writing an opening sentence on one and tossing it out to the class. Have them continue passing the ball by adding the next sentence to it and tossing it again . . . keep the ball rolling and the story growing as it goes from one to another!

Beach-Ball Letters

Great for little ones, and so versatile! Write letters on the ball and toss it to a child. Where their hands land they will see a letter; the object is to quickly call out a word that starts with that letter. As the game progresses, you can intensify the challenge by asking for verbs, nouns, adverbs, prepositions, adjectives, etc. You can also have them tell a quick story using an object that begins with that letter; maybe grab an hourglass timer and have them tell the story as quickly as possible, racing the sand!

Character Creations

Show random pictures of people; have your students develop characters from the images. You may need to help your students look for distinguishing characteristics that make each character unusual. Look at their eyes--what do they see? What conclusions can they draw from looking into the eyes of another person? Joy, sadness, loneliness, despair, light? Is there a story in their face? In their hands? In the clothing they wear? You may need to continue prompting thoughts if necessary. There are no wrong answers, and all ideas can be explored.

Raising Voices

Create character names, ages, and occupations. Assign a character to each student and have them work together in groups of two or three to create stories. Have them stand together, introduce their character, and begin developing their stories aloud in their small groups. This allows them to think on the spot and to work with twists and turns as the other characters involved add to the story.

Punctuation Stories

Choose a paragraph from the book you are reading, or a story you know, or a newspaper article. Copy the punctuation marks from it and try to write the beginning of a story using those same punctuation marks in the same order your found them. Need an example?

Here you go: . , , , . ! " ," .. ? .

Capitalization Stories

Do the same as you did above with the Punctuation Stories, but this time copy the capital letters only and try to write the beginning of a story using those same capital letters in the same order you found them. Here's another quick example for you to try:

S T C I A M M R O N

Roll-of-the-Dice Story Titles

Start by creating a set of story possibilities--check out the example below for ideas. You will need two dice--tossing will determine the story assignment for each player. Each player will roll the dice twice, and the first number will determine the beginning of the title with the second roll concluding the title. Have each player create their story and then take turns sharing!

First Throw:

2 – My Granny's 3 – The Hero's 4 – My Enemy's 5 – The Nutcracker's 6 – My Pet Giraffe's 7 – An Old Tree's 8 – My Tricycle's 9 – The Neighbor's 10 – The Firemen's 11 – The Bright Star's 12 – The Stinky Shoe's

Second Throw:

2 – Secret 3 – Reward 4 – Plan for Success 5 – Problem 6 – Best Friend 7- Dream 8 – Biggest Worry 9 – Finest Hour 10 – Surprise Birthday Party 11- Crazy Past 12 – Audacious Goal

So, if you were to roll an 8 for your first throw and a 9 for your second throw, your title would be "My Tricycle's Finest Hour." Or, a 6 on your first throw and a 10 for the second would make your title, "My Pet Giraffe's Surprise

Birthday Party." Feel free to come up with as many ideas as possible, and see what kinds of crazy creations come from these fun titles!

Get Out of Here

This is a fun game I like to play right before the end of the day or right before lunch. Stand ready with a set of "Trivial Pursuit" questions or flashcards; preferably something you've been studying or working on in your studies already. In order to get out, the kids need to answer three questions correctly. If not, they head to the back of the line and start over.

Jeopardy

This is such a fun game and is perfect for studying geography, history, the arts, science, history, novels . . . The list goes on and on and on! It can be a perfect tool to use for studying for tests, finals, or for the end of a unit or unit study.

There are plenty of free "Jeopardy" templates for teachers available online. This helps make prep-time a bit more manageable. OR have your students use designing a "Jeopardy" game as one of their projects! The bonus is that through their research, they will master the material and be ready to share their new-found knowledge with others! It's a game easily tailored to all ages.

Student-Made Games

Who doesn't like to showcase their skills, knowledge, or talents? Put your students to work helping to create some fabulous games; it is likely that every single game listed on these pages could be created by the kids in your life! Challenge them to stump you with their questions and content!

As you can see, learning doesn't ever need to be dull or boring! With a small amount of effort and creative thinking, we can enrich education by helping students fully embrace and love what this amazing world holds for them!

Happy Learning!

Ten

Lists, Lists, Lists!!!

Awesome Adjectives!

Adjectives: Simply put, adjectives are descriptive words that modify nouns. This is one that makes me a bit crazy! Too often, our Awesome Adjective friends come under fire for their cluttering quality, but often it's quality--not quantity--that is the issue. In my opinion, adjectives add to ALL writing, and I teach and preach the use of them whenever and wherever possible! When you find just the right word for the job, there is nothing that satisfies so well. Check out a list of some of my very favorites, and be sure to have these available to spark ideas:

gooey, heroic, blurry, adamant, selective, fuzzy, tangy, fluffy, inspired, scrumptious, fanciful, antic, boorish, caustic, intense, clever, bewildered, colossal, peculiar, comely, effulgent, wretched, witty, sparkling, brilliant, zany, ferocious, zealous, courageous, curious, meticulous, insidious, contemptuous, limpid, transparent, luminous, dynamic, valiant, rambunctious, confident, daring, opulent, sour, vivacious, murky, quaint, stupendous, frigid, ecstatic, mysterious, inquisitive, bold, exuberant, wistful, remarkable, energetic, determined, dubious, graceful, clumsy, awkward, nimble, clever, dull, obtuse, meek, frightened, timid, vigilant, cautious, capable, adequate, absent-minded, adventurous, daring, indifferent, apologetic, hideous, horrid, dreadful, ghastly, revolting, nasty, cruel, cheeky, obnoxious, disrespectful, contrary, ornery, subtle, optimistic, courageous, cowardly, gullible, arrogant, haughty, naïve, curious, stubborn, brazen, modest, humble, proud, dishonest, righteous, greedy, wise, tricky, loyal, relaxed, tranquil, lazy, rambunctious, crazy, erratic, fidgety, lively, still, famished, surprised, startled, sullen, terrified, furious, annoyed, groggy, alert, tense, cranky, gloomy, irritable, lonely, exhausted, cheerful, delighted, blithe, content, carefree, demanding, challenging, effortless, fantastic, marvelous, splendid, brilliant, superb, striking, stunning, gorgeous, picturesque, lovely, charming, enchanting, delicate, pleasant, darling, monstrous, immense, enormous, massive, mammoth, brawny, bulky, towering, cavernous, puny, minute, microscopic, petite, slight, bitter, frosty, sweltering, scorching, blistering, muggy, stifling, oppressive, cozy, comfy, eternal, ceaseless, perpetual, endless, temporary, intimidating, menacing, miserable, dangerous, delinquent, vile, quarrel some, hostile, malicious, savage, stern, somber, mysterious, shocking, infamous, ingenious, thrifty, generous, prudent, stingy, spoiled, anxious, nervous, impatient, worried, excited, courteous, compassionate, benevolent, polite, amusing, precise, eccentric, whimsical, lavish, edgy, trendy, rancid, foul, filthy, repulsive, lousy, fluttering, soaring, sparkling, gilded, glowing, gaunt, sloppy, serious, grave, intense, severe, absurd, sluggish, dawdling, meandering, scarce, copious, muffled, lulling, creaky, shrill, piercing, slimy, grimy, mangy, swollen, parched, crispy, spiky, slick, slippery, plush, wrinkly, glassy, snug, abundant, substantial, yummy, victorious, thankful, joyous, raspy, blunt, petulant, laughable, tenacious, turbulent, pompous, voracious, withering . . . to name a few.

Prepositions:

These are the words that show or indicate location. Super-fun to play with (especially with younger kids) if you call out prepositions or prepositional phrases and get them moving! Some examples are:

aboard, about, above, across, after, against, along, among, around, at, before, behind, below, beneath, beside, between, beyond, by, concerning, down, during, except, from, in, inside, into, like, near, of, off, on, out, over, past, since, through, throughout, till, to, toward, under, underneath, until, up, upon, with, within, without.

Vivacious Verbs:

Verbs are essential in every sentence we speak and write. In fact, try saying something, or anything out loud without using a verb--you can't. Verbs are so important that a sentence can't exist without one! In fact, a verb doesn't even need any other part of speech to form a complete sentence--it can form a one-word sentence such as, "Run!" "Go." "Swim." "Laugh!" "STOP!" Need a fantastic list? Read this:

aspire, exaggerate, boast, consider, quench, devour, digest, dine, drain, gorge, guzzle, indulge, inhale, slurp, nibble, announce, comment, declare, utter, gasp, huff, sigh, snap, snicker, express, bellow, holler, howl, lament, shriek, wail, moan, groan, blabber, bluster, gush, scoff, snuffle, squeal, inquire, implore, plead, instruct, demand, encourage, impress, manipulate, persuade, insult, leach, neglect, outrage, overrule, pacify, confuse, confound, dazzle, deceive, conceal, crave, desire, imagine, exhaust, excite, ignite, petrify, startle, deter, forbid, halt, chase, follow, obey, pursue, arrive, exit, journey, traverse, venture, ascend, mount, scale, burrow, sink, assault, disarm, cleave, dismantle, corrupt, ruin, craft, create, design, manufacture, gel, liquefy, brew, extract, alter, evolve, modify, morph, enjoy, relish, gloat, wallow, adore, amuse, cherish, treasure, despise, loathe, dwell, occupy, admire, gaze, peek, peer, bargain, deal, plot, conspire, cascade, flow, spatter, spew, sprinkle, float, glide, cast, catapult, hurl, lob, nudge, jab, poke, smudge, stroke, loaf, lounge, amble, creep, dawdle, lope, stagger, bolt, flounce, stroll, stride, meander, plod, saunter, stalk, wander, scurry, adorn, flourish, fascinate, warp, prance, scamper, dash, volunteer, magnify, whimper, discover, savor, flutter, chortle, contemplate, improvise, ooze, advise, captivate, chatter, accentuate, pursue, treasure, divulge, ponder, soar, wish.

Adverbs:

These tell us how, when, where, or how much! An adverb is a part of speech that describes or modifies a verb, adjective, or another adverb. Modify simply means to add to or change the meaning of a word.

Spotting an adverb is pretty easy business--when you see a word that ends in "-ly", it is probably an adverb! Here are a few to check out:

financially, willfully, abruptly, endlessly, firmly, delightfully, quickly, lightly, eternally, delicately, wearily, sorrowfully, beautifully, truthfully.

Again, adverbs tell us how, when, where, and how much. Here are a few great examples of those, specifically:

How? quickly, sadly, slowly, boldly, happily, timidly, sloppily, briskly, randomly, wholeheartedly, expertly, cheerfully, uneasily

When? early, today, yesterday, always, sometimes, tomorrow, now, first, last, later, regularly, often, never, monthly, usually

Where? here, there, inside, upstairs, nowhere, outside, everywhere, somewhere, underground, downstairs

How much? very, completely, almost, partly, nearly, really, too, only, also, enough, quite, so, rather

Antonyms, Synonyms and Homonyms . . . Oh, My!!!

Antonyms are words with opposite meanings to other words. *Synonyms* are words that have the same or nearly the same meaning as some other words. *Homonyms* are words that are pronounced the same, and are sometimes spelled the same, but have *different meanings*. A few helpful lists are below:

Antonym Examples:

Achieve – Fail

Idle – Active

Afraid – Confident

Ancient – Modern

Arrive – Depart

Arrogant – Humble

Ascend – Descend

Attack – Defend

Blunt – Sharp

Brave – Cowardly

Cautious – Careless

Complex – Simple

Compliment – Insult

Insane – Sane

Crooked – Straight

Decrease – Increase

Abundance – Lack

Destroy – Create

Divide – Unite

Expand – Contract

Freeze - Thaw/Melt

Full – Empty

Generous – Stingy

Giant – Miniscule/Minuscule

Gloomy – Cheerful

Guilty – Innocent

Hire – Fire

Include – Exclude

Individual – Group

Innocent – Guilty

Knowledge – Ignorance

Liquid – Solid

Sparse – Crowded

Major – Minor

Marvelous – Terrible

Mature – Immature

Maximum - Minimum

Noisy – Quiet

Optimist - Pessimist

Ordinary – Extraordinary

Partial – Complete

Passive – Active

Stable – Unstable

Plentiful – Scarce

Positive – Negative

Strong – Weak

Praise – Criticism

Private – Public

Problem – Solution

Professional – Amateur

Profit – Loss

Superiority – Inferiority

Random – Specific

Inflexible – Flexible

Segregate – Integrate

Simple - Complicated/Complex

Stiff – Flexible

Strength - Weakness

Sunny - Overcast

Temporary – Permanent

Timid – Bold

Toward – Away

Tragic – Comic

Transparent - Opaque

Triumph – Defeat

Union – Separation

Unique – Common

Upset – Calm

Urge – Deter

Vacant – Occupied

Vague – Definite

Vertical – Horizontal

Villain – Hero

Visible - Invisible

Wax - Wane

Wealth – Poverty

Synonym Examples:

enormous, huge, gigantic, massive

fertile, fruitful, abundant, productive

benefit, profit, revenue, yield

house, dwelling, abode, domicile

intelligent, clever, brilliant, knowledgeable

loyal, faithful, ardent, devoted

annihilation, destruction, carnage, extermination

organization, institution, management

partner, associate, colleague, companion

polite, courteous, cordial, gracious

risky, dangerous, perilous, treacherous

sleepy, drowsy, listless, sluggish

destitute, poor, bankrupt, impoverished

cunning, keen, sharp, sly

Homonym Examples:

Aid - Aide

Affect - Effect

Aisle - I'll - Isle

Aloud - Allowed

Altar - Alter

Ark - Arc

Ball - Bawl

Base - Bass

Beech - Beach

Birth - Berth

Bore - Boar

Byte - Bite

Blew - Blue

Bow - Bough

Boy - Buoy

Bread - Bred

Browse - Brows

Cell - Sell

Cereal - Serial

Chilly - Chili

Chord - Cord

Complement - Compliment

Counsel - Council

Creak - Creek

Crews - Cruise

Dual - Duel

Fair - Fare

Fairy - Ferry

Feat - Feet

Fir - Fur

Flea - Flee

Gorilla - Guerrilla

Grease - Greece

Groan - Grown

Hall - Haul

Halve - Have

Holey - Holy - Wholly

Incite - Insight

Jeans - Genes

Knead - Need

Knight - Night

Lessen - Lesson

Links - Lynx

Loan - Lone

Oral - Aural

Ought - Aught

Oar - Or - Ore

Overdo - Overdue

Peak - Peek

Phase - Faze

Pole - Poll

Pray - Prey

Principal - Principle

Real - Reel

Ring - Wring

Role - Roll

Sew - So - Sow

Site - Sight - Cite

Soar - Sore

Sole - Soul

Toe - Tow

Vary - Very

Wail - Whale

Wait - Weight

We - Wee

Weather - Whether

Which - Witch

Whose - Who's

99 of The Most Misspelled Words

In the English Language

Give your kiddos a head start and help them master this list!

acceptable

accidentally

accommodate

acquire

allot

amateur

apparent

argument

atheist

believe

bellwether

calendar

cemetery

changeable

collectible

column

committed

conscience

conscientious

conscious

consensus

daiquiri

definite

discipline

drunkenness

dumbbell

embarrass

equipment

exhilarate

exceed

existence

experience

fiery

foreign

gauge

grateful

guarantee

harass

height

hierarchy

humorous

ignorance

immediate

independent

indispensable

inoculate

intelligence

jewelry

judgment

kernel

leisure

liaison

library

license

lightning

maintenance

maneuver

medieval

memento

millennium

miniature

minuscule

mischievous

misspell

neighbor

noticeable

occasionally

occurrence

pastime

perseverance

personnel

playwright

possession

precede

principal– head; as a school principal

principle– a rule

privilege

pronunciation

publicly

questionnaire

receive

recommend

refer

relevant

restaurant

rhyme

rhythm

schedule

separate

sergeant

supersede

their

threshold

twelfth

tyranny

until

vacuum

weather

weird

About the Author

Stacey is a passionate educator, speaker and author!

She has been in education for over twenty years, working primarily with children and the youth. She has also spent much of that time homeschooling her own seven children, empowering women and youth, working on teacher development projects and parent education. She loves coordinating events of all sizes and is responsible for the formation of several learning cooperatives. Stacey is the author of a Life-Changing Christmas Tale, titled *The Glitter Keeper* and author of an educator's book entitled *FUNology*.   Stacey is the Program Director of a large elective-day program for school-aged children, where she is known as *Miss Stacey*.

To capture the true essence of Stacey, picture a woman flying by the seat of her pants, chocolate in hand. Stacey skips through life, dabbling in a little of this and a little of that, forever exploring and embracing new passions and dreams. It's not uncommon to see her rocking out in her favorite little yellow slug-bug convertible--screeching to sudden stops, jumping out, camera in hand, snapping shots of sunflowers along the road, breathtaking sunsets, or a dilapidated barn.

Stacey's greatest joy is being the Mom to a handful-and-a-half of children. She spends her days right alongside them learning and experiencing all this life has to offer. Milkshake dates with her very own Knight in Shining Armor are a weekly treat, and a lifesaver in this crazy and amazing life!

If she had one wish come true, she would cover the whole world with glitter in the hope of spreading light and joy for all.

www.ingramcontent.com/pod-product-compliance
Lightning Source LLC
Chambersburg PA
CBHW060819050426

42449CB00008B/1729